# This book belongs to:

_____

© Copyright 2021-2025- All rights reserved.

You may not reproduce, duplicate or send the contents of this book without direct written permission from the author. You cannot hereby despite any circumstance blame the publisher or hold him or her to legal responsibility for any reparation, compensations, or monetary forfeiture owing to the information included herein, either in a direct or an indirect way.

Legal Notice: This book has copyright protection. You can use the book for personal purpose. You should not sell, use, alter, distribute, quote, take excerpts or paraphrase in part or whole the material contained in this book without obtaining the permission of the author first.

Disclaimer Notice: You must take note that the information in this document is for casual reading and entertainment purposes only. We have made every attempt to provide accurate, up to date and reliable information. We do not express or imply guarantees of any kind. The persons who read admit that the writer is not occupied in giving legal, financial, medical or other advice. We put this book content by sourcing various places.

Please consult a licensed professional before you try any techniques shown in this book. By going through this document, the book lover comes to an agreement that under no situation is the author accountable for any forfeiture, direct or indirect, which they may incur because of the use of material contained in this document, including, but not limited to, —errors, omissions, or inaccuracies.

# Sight Noun Words with Fingerspelling

**apple**

**baby**

**back**

**ball**

**bear**

**bed**

**bell**

**bird**

**birthday**

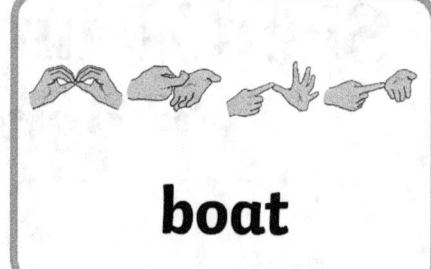
**boat**

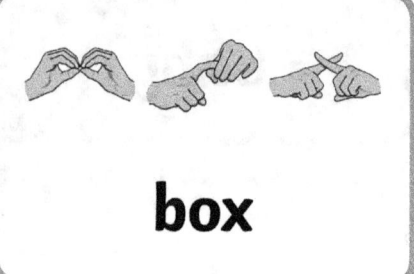
**box**

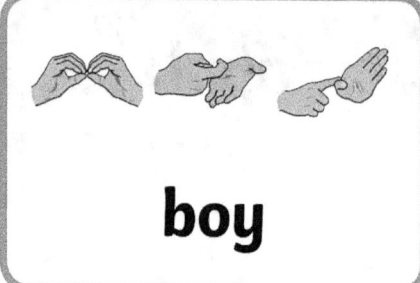
**boy**

**bread**

**brother**

**cake**

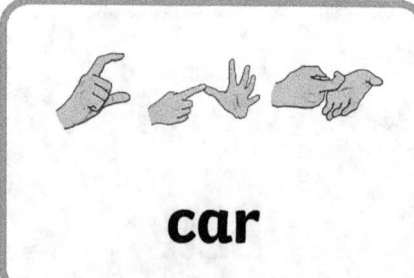
**car**

**Christmas**

coat

corn

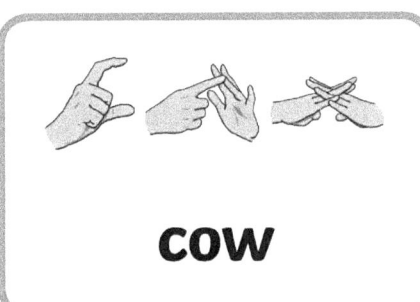
cow

**cat**

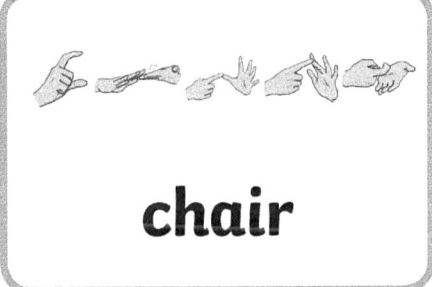
**chair**

**chicken**

**children**

day

dog

doll

door

duck

egg

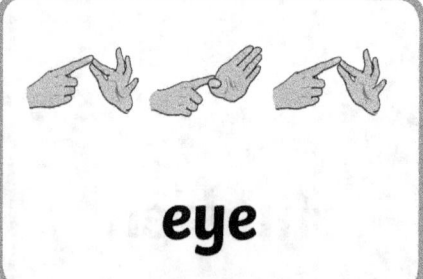
eye

farm

farmer

father

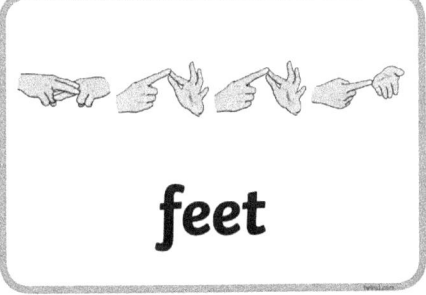
feet

fire

fish

floor

flower

game

ground

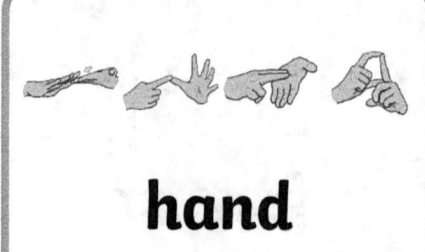
hand

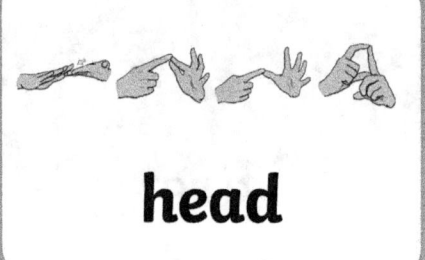
head

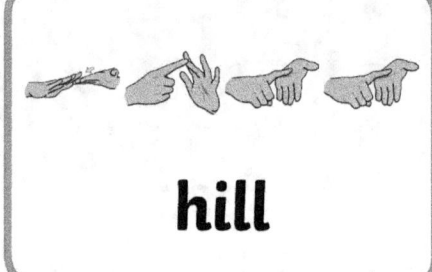
hill

garden

girl

goodbye

grass

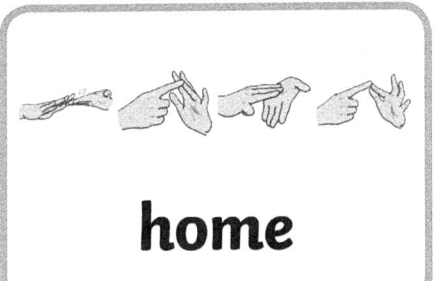
home

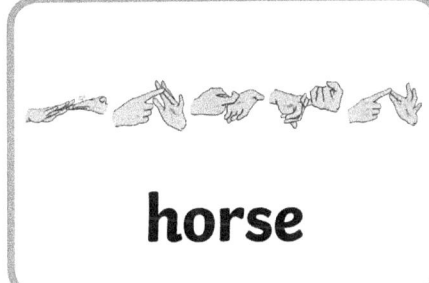
horse

house

kitty

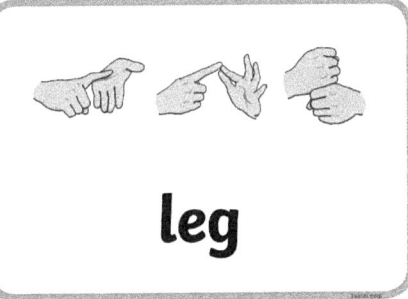
leg

letter

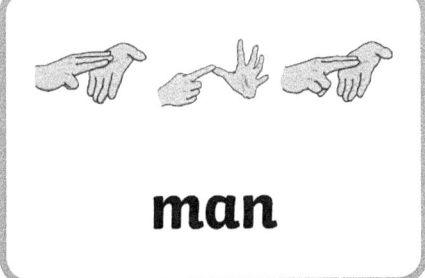
man

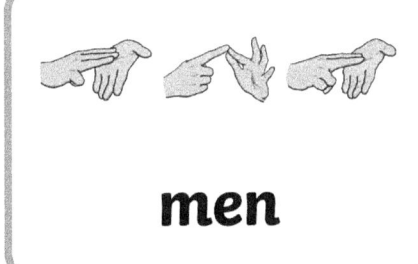
men

**milk**

**monkey**

**morning**

**mother**

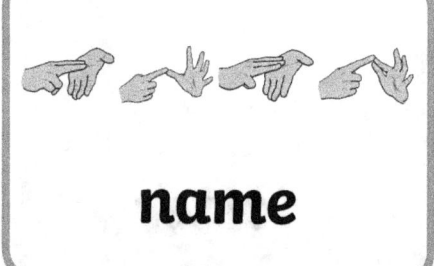

**name**

**nest**

**night**

**paper**

**rain**

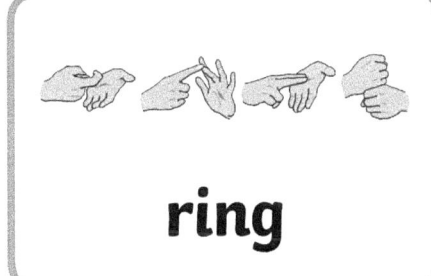
**ring**

**robin**

**Santa Claus**

**party**

**picture**

**pig**

**rabbit**

school

seed

sheep

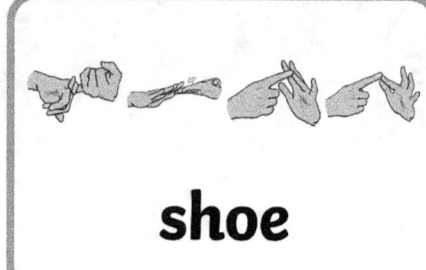
shoe

sister

snow

song

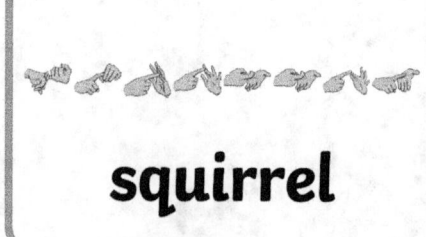
squirrel

**stick**

**street**

**sun**

**table**

**thing**

**time**

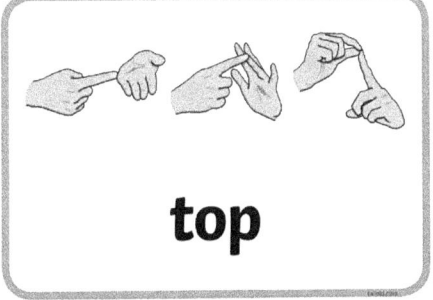

**top**

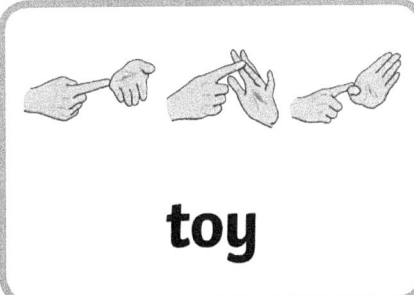

**toy**

tree

watch

water

way

wind

window

wood

# Fingerspelling Phase 2 Practice High-Frequency Words

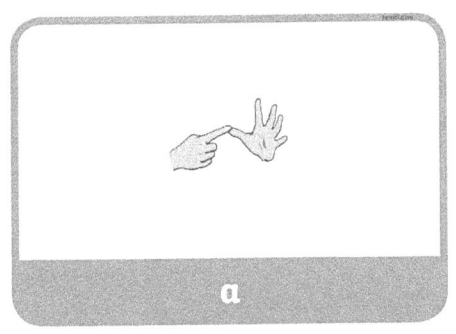
a

dad

I

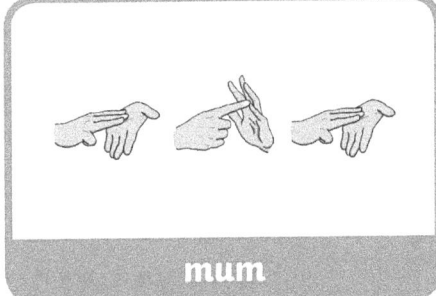
mum

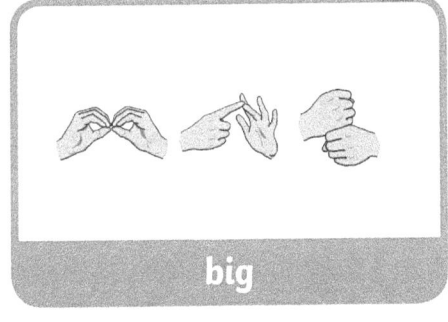
big

it

at

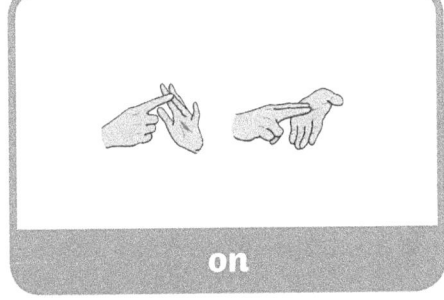
on

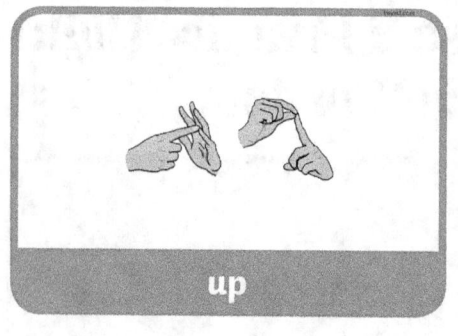
up

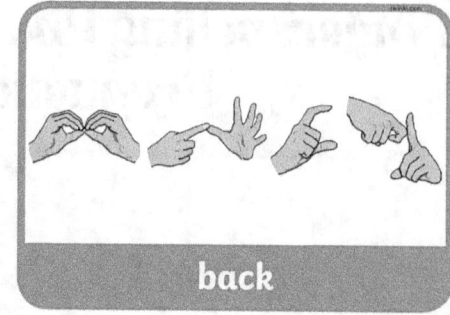
back

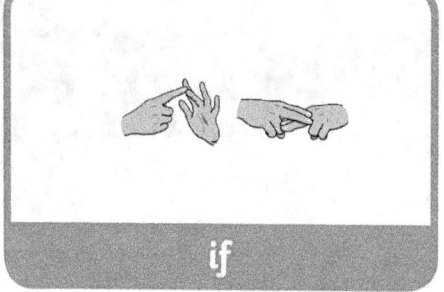
if

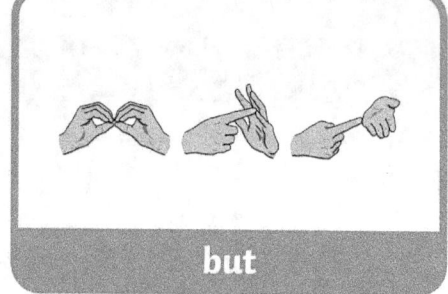
but

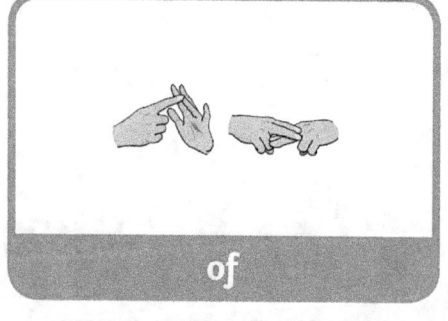
of

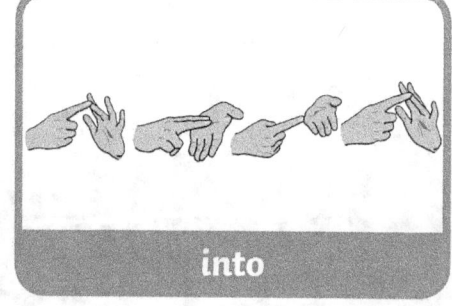
into

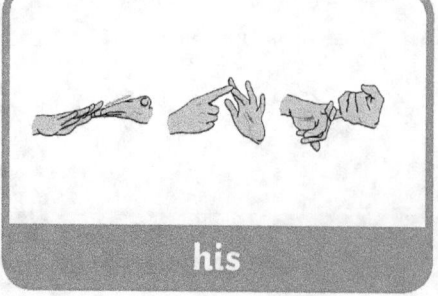
his

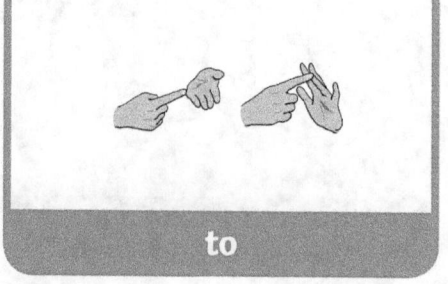
to

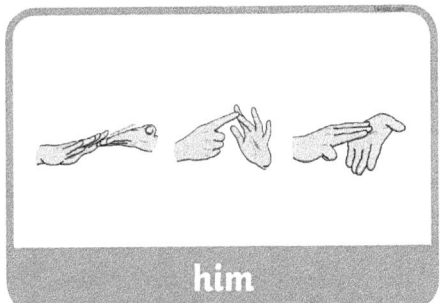
him

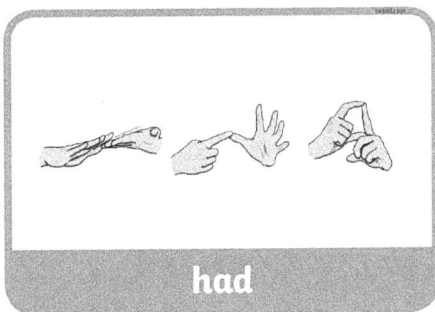
had

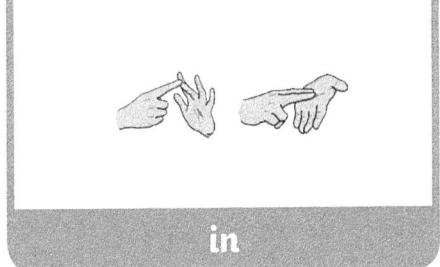
in

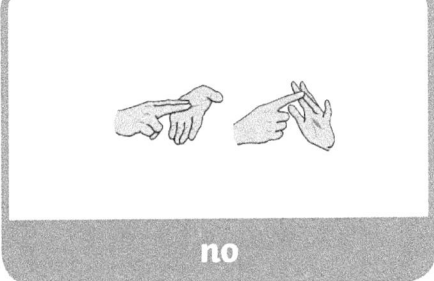
no

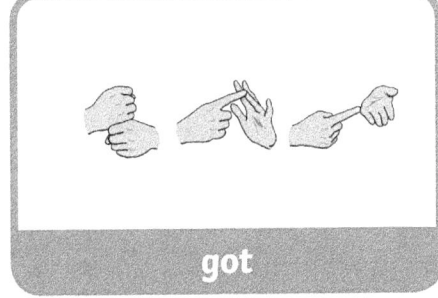
got

go

an

as

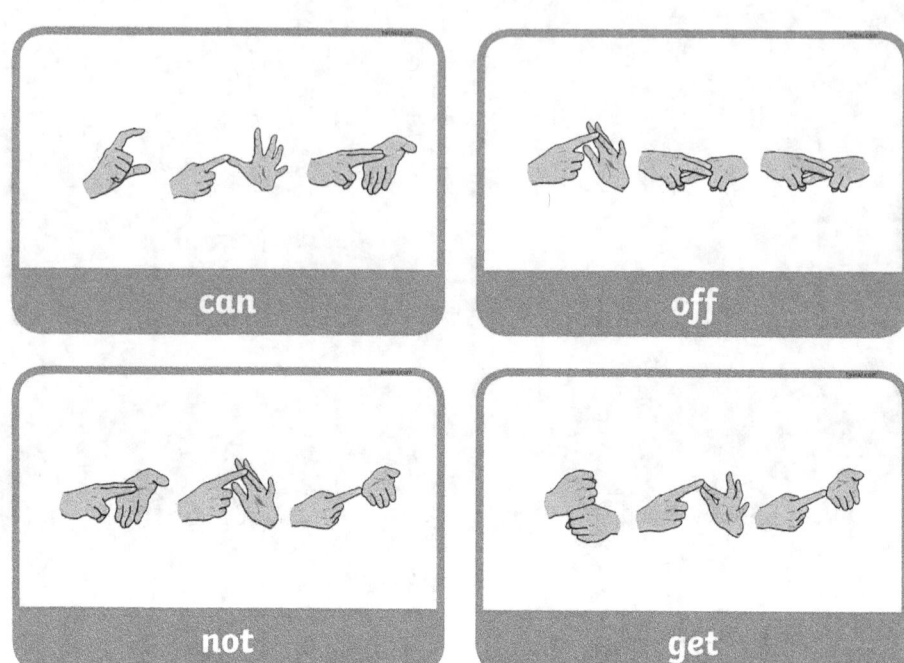

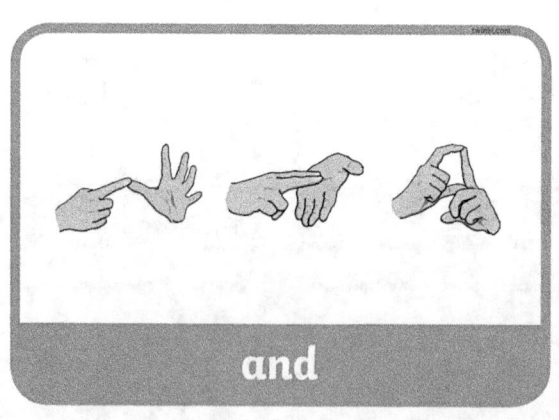

# Fingerspelling Phase 3 Practice High-Frequency Words

will

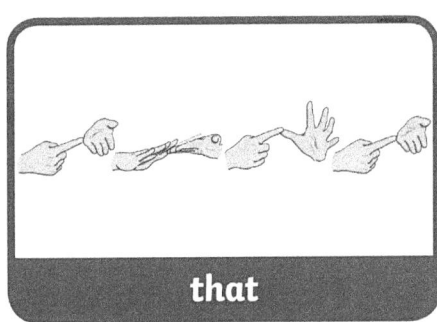
that

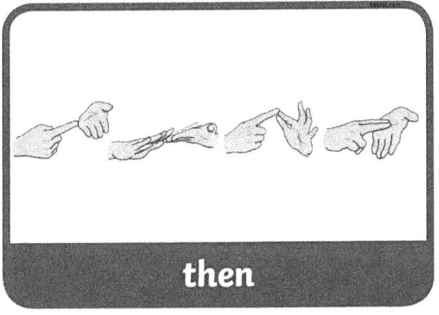
then

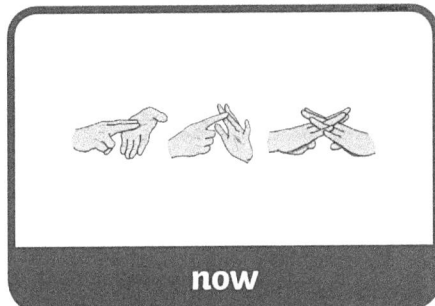
now

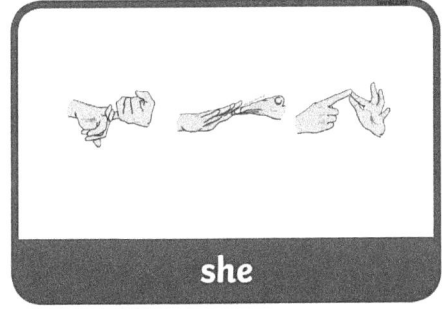
she

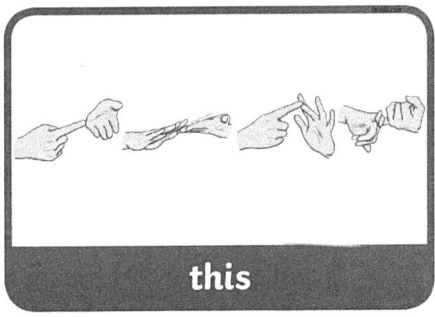
this

with

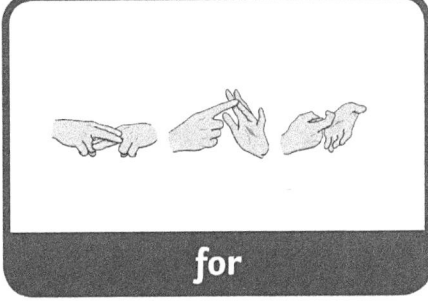
for

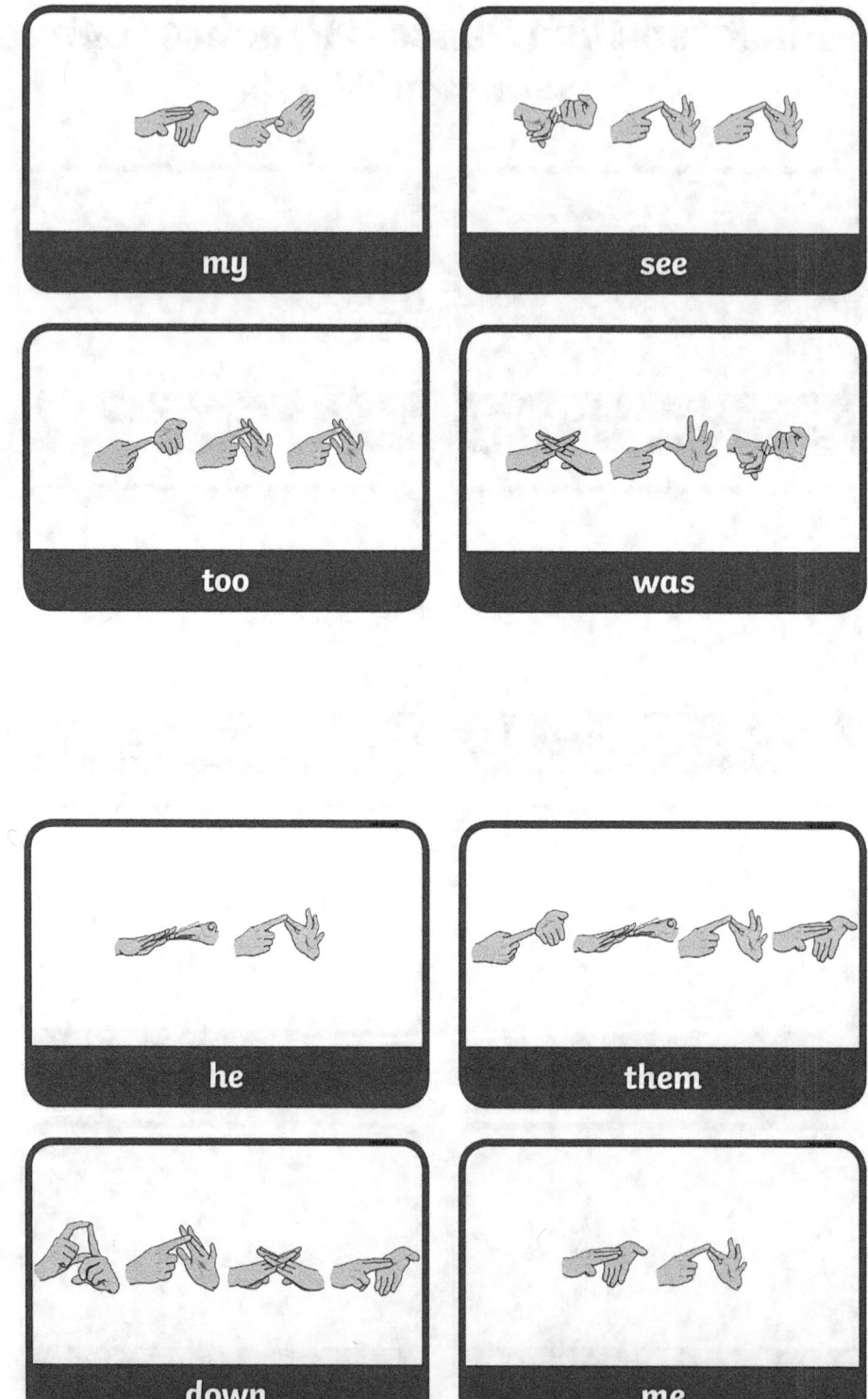

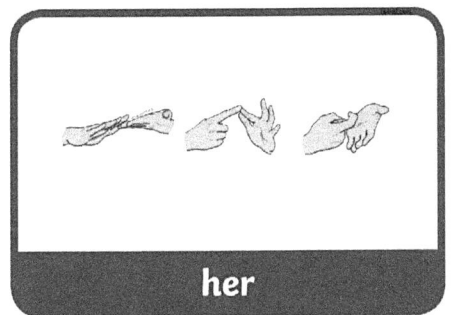
her

be

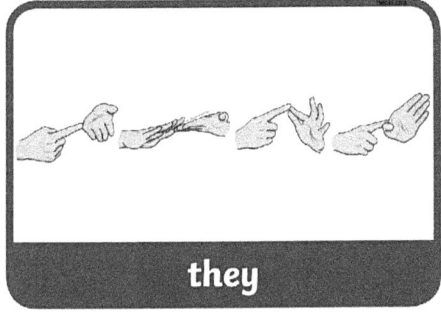
they

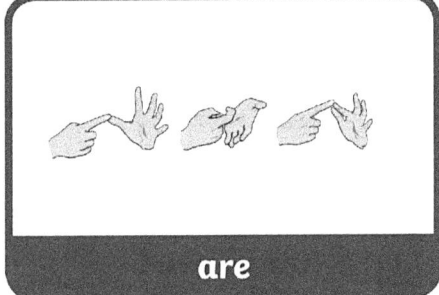
are

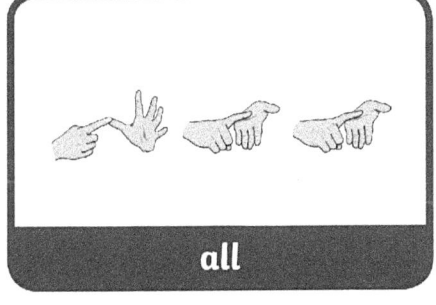
all

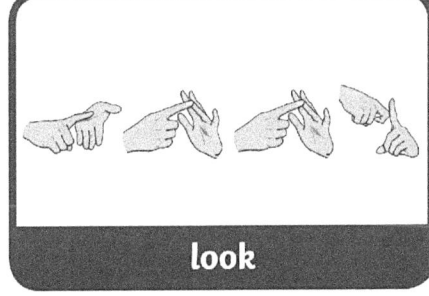
look

we

you

# Fingerspelling Phase 4 Practice
# High-Frequency Words

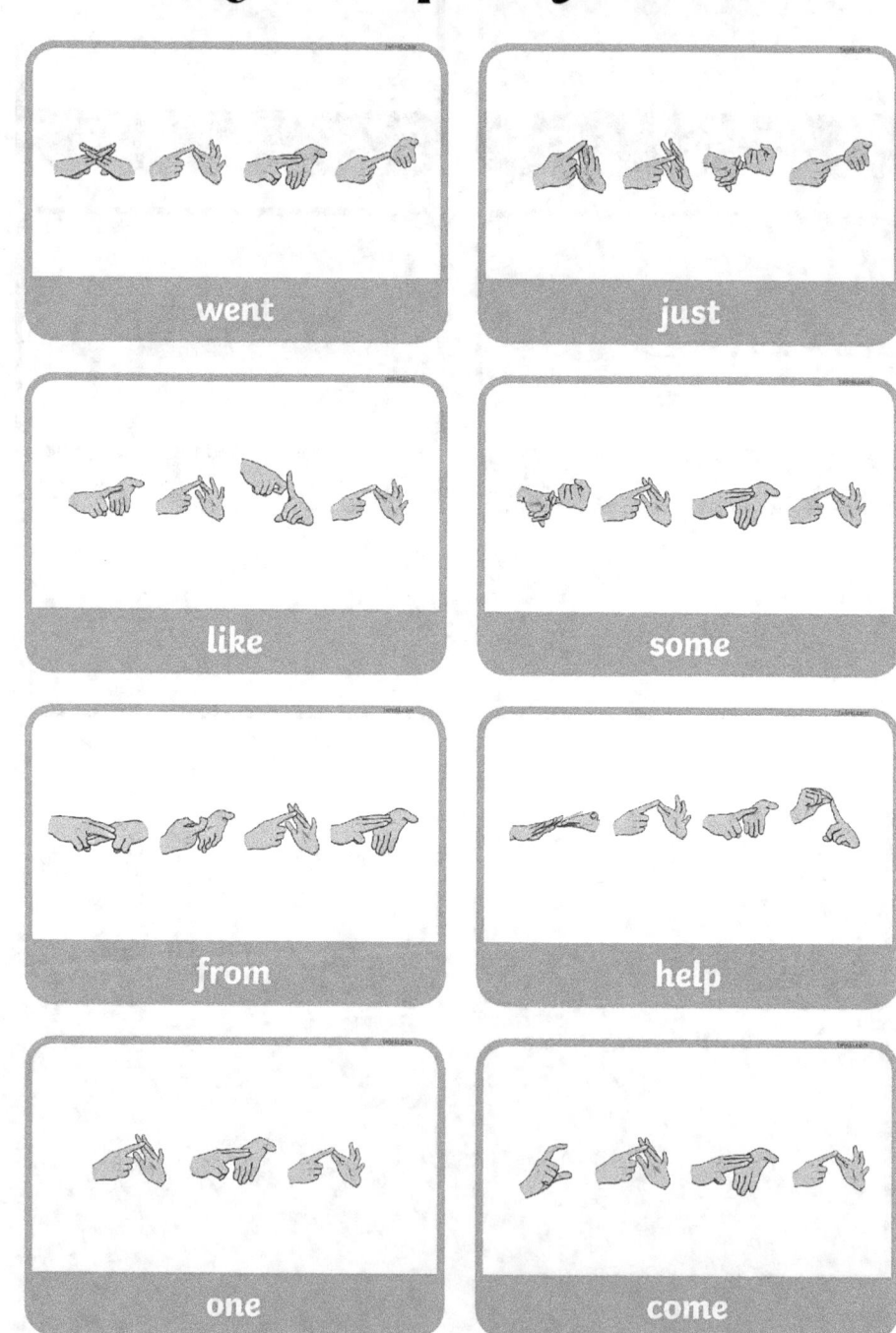

little

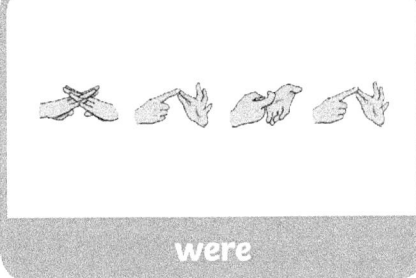
were

do

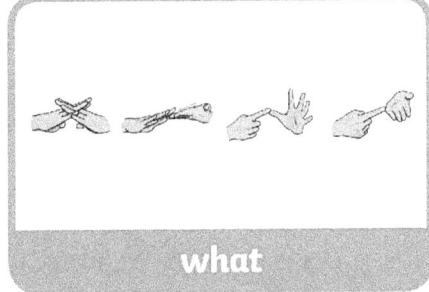
what

children

said

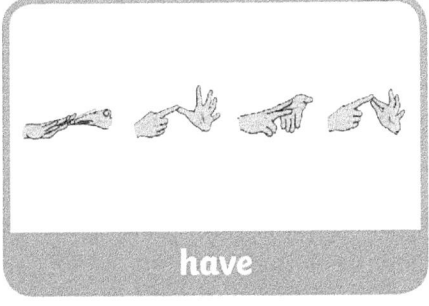
have

there

# Fingerspelling Phase 5 Practice High-Frequency Words

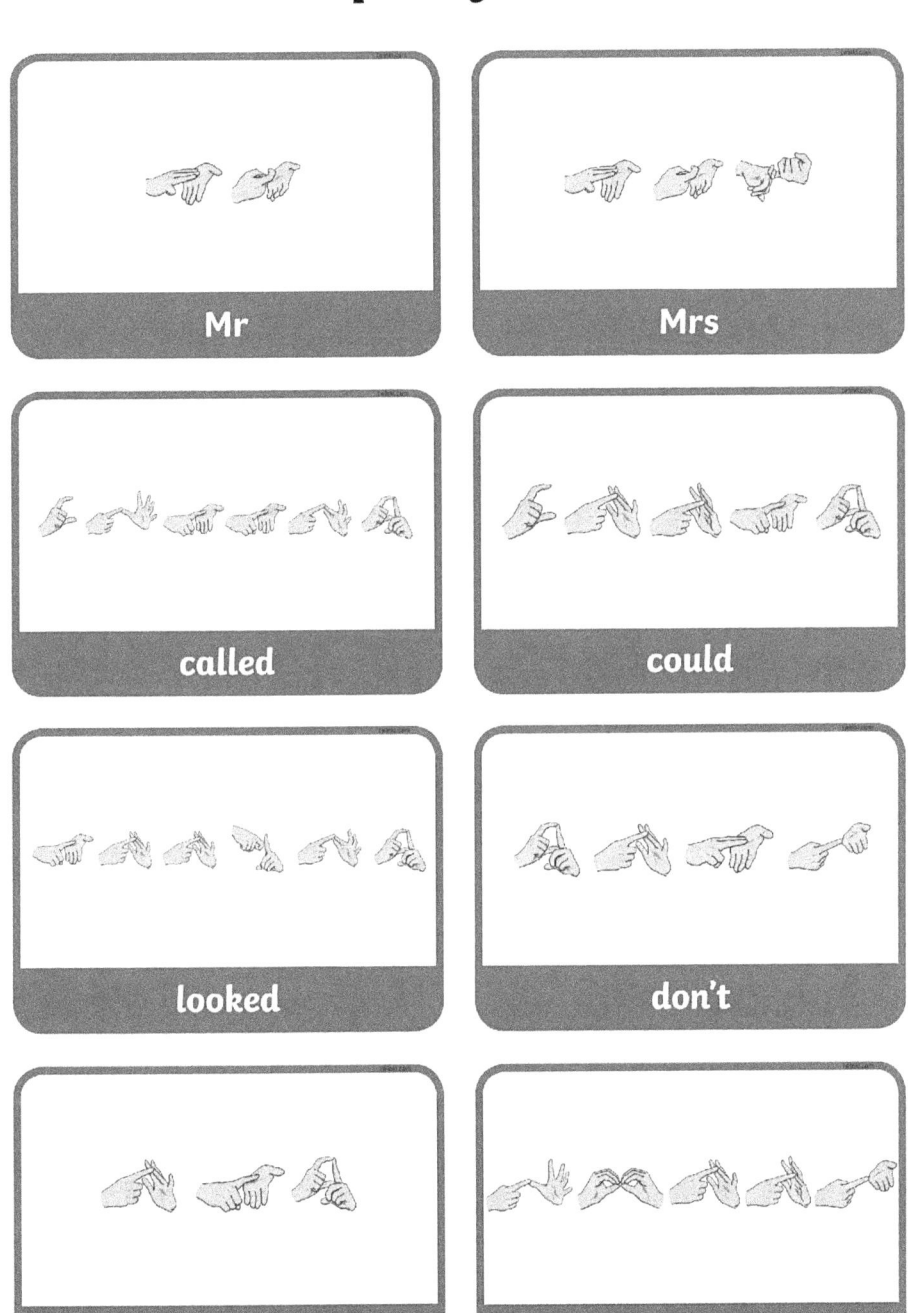

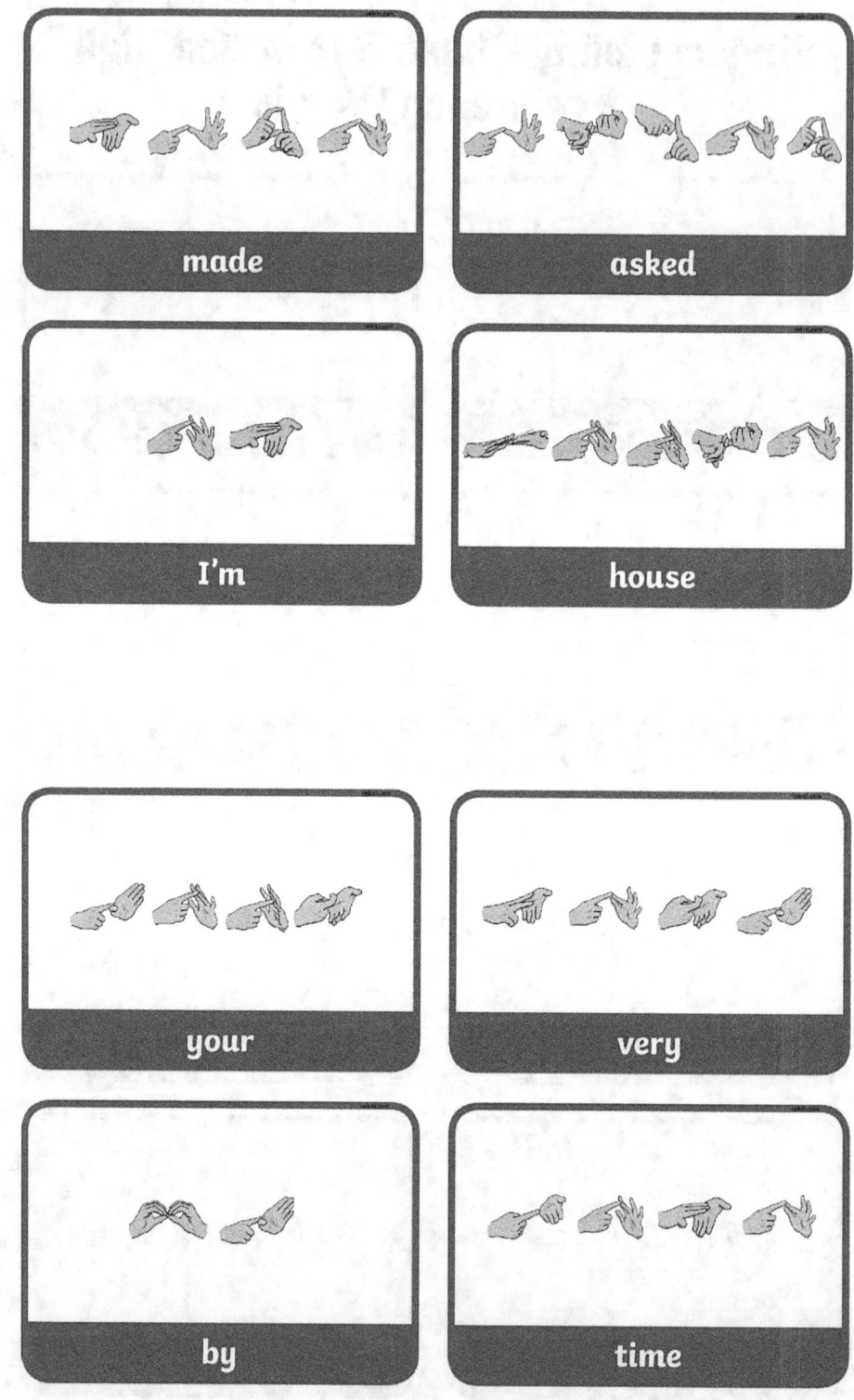

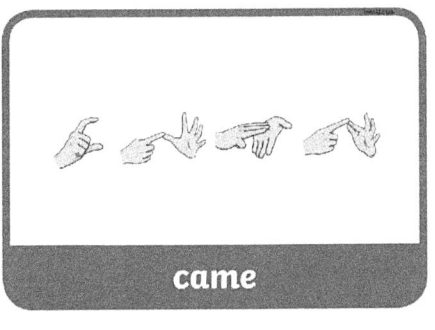
came

make

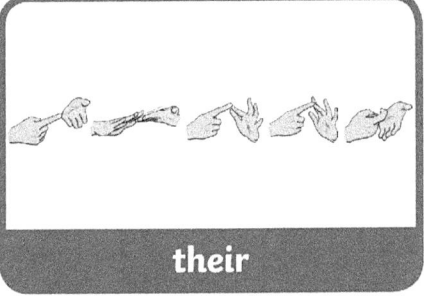
their

day

saw

put

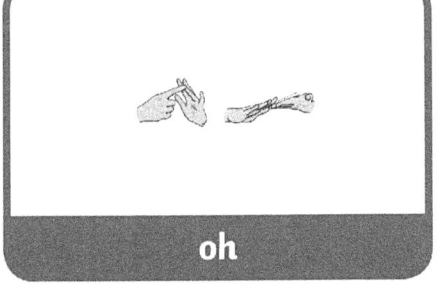
oh

people

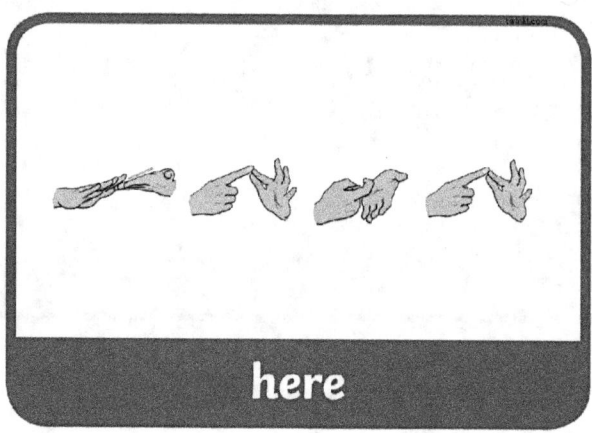

# Pre Primer Dolch List Sight Words with Fingerspelling

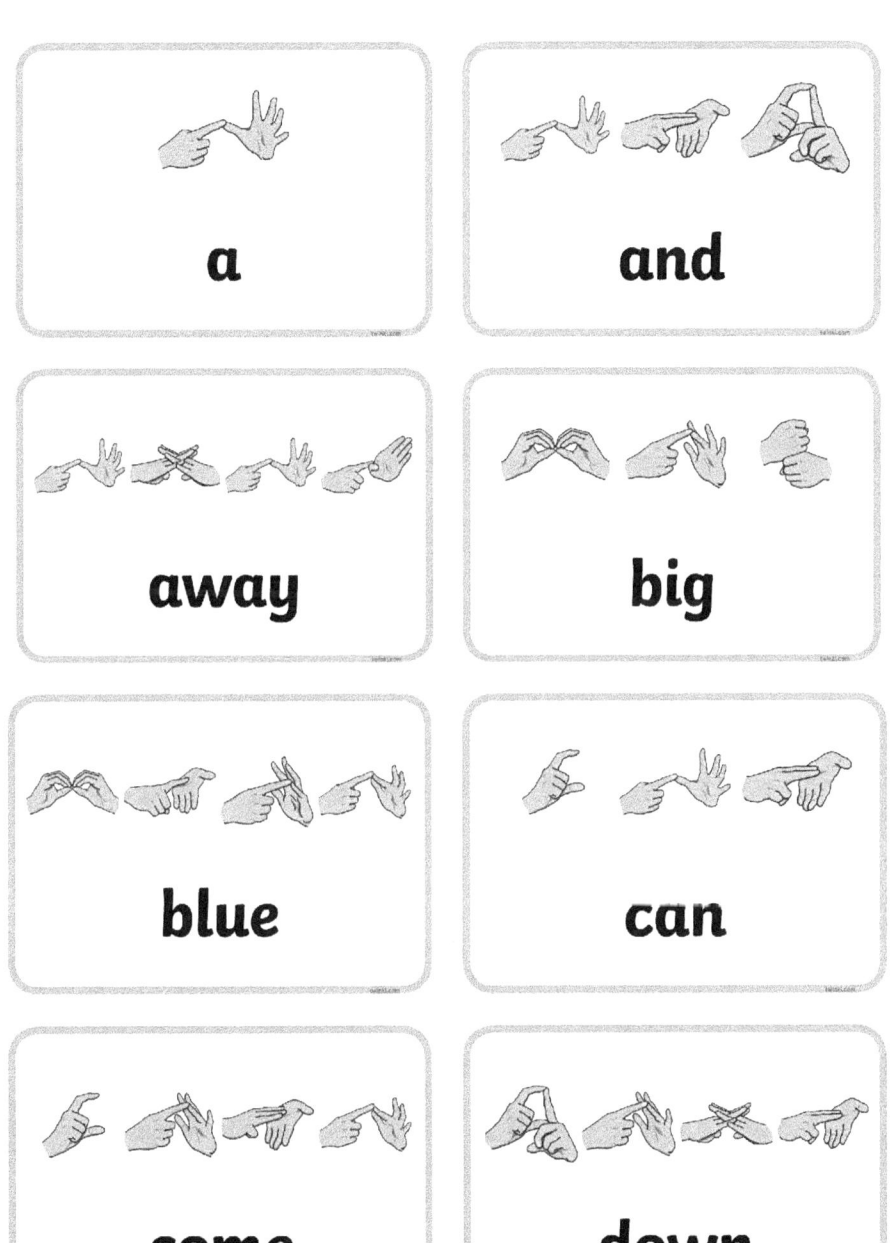

find

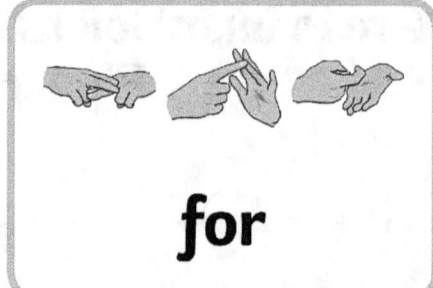
for

funny

go

help

here

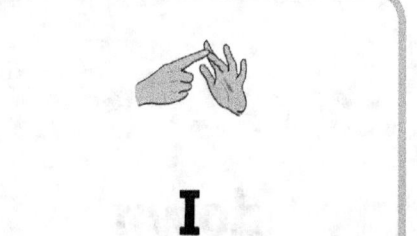
I

in

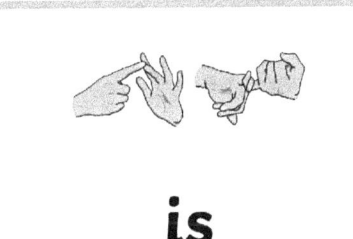
**is**

**it**

**jump**

**little**

**look**

**make**

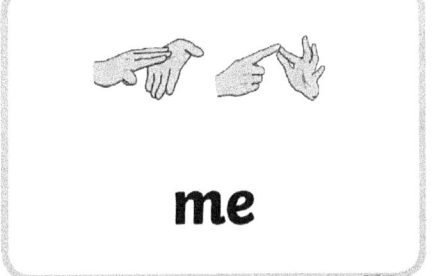
**me**

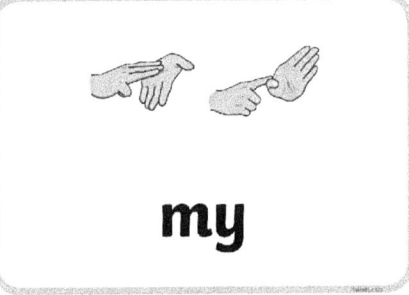
**my**

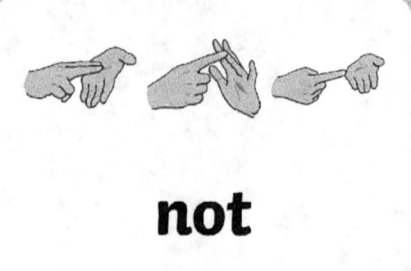

**not**

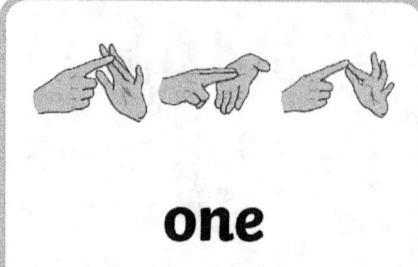

**one**

**play**

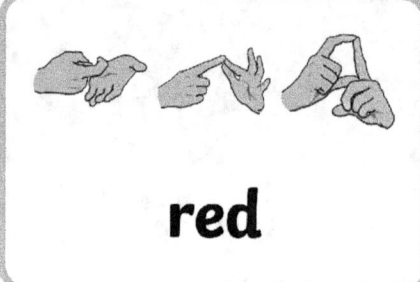

**red**

**run**

**said**

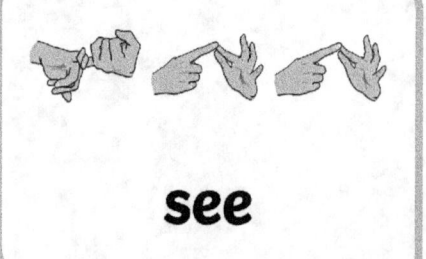

**see**

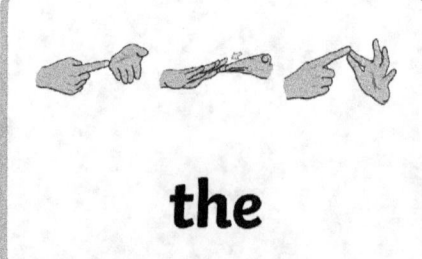

**the**

we

where

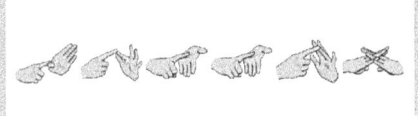
yellow

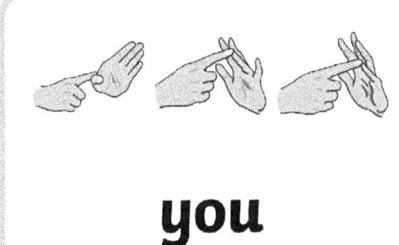
you

three

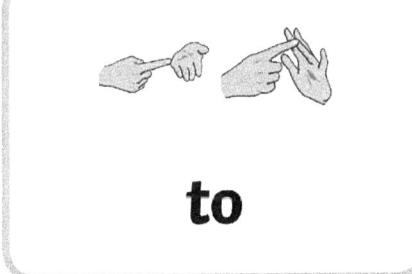
to

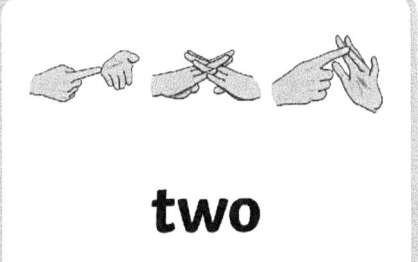
two

up

# Primer Dolch List Sight Words with Fingerspelling

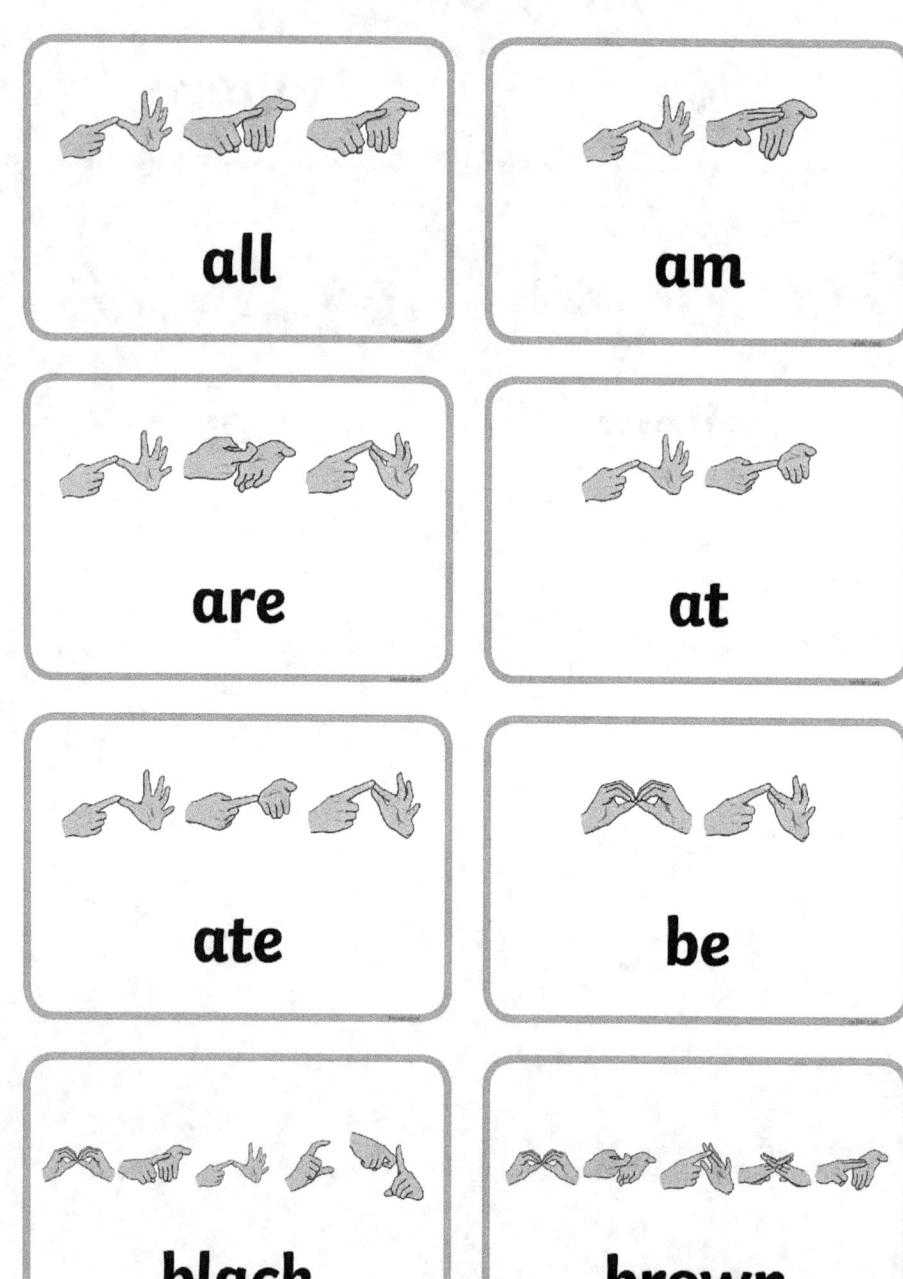

**but**

**came**

**did**

**do**

**eat**

**four**

**get**

**good**

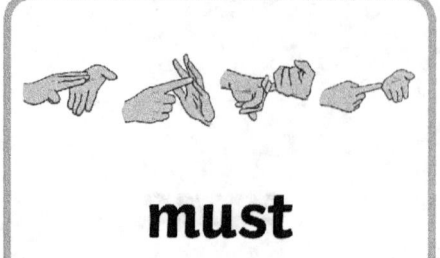
must

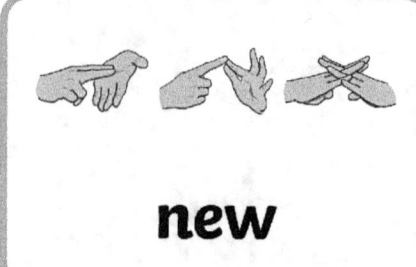
new

no

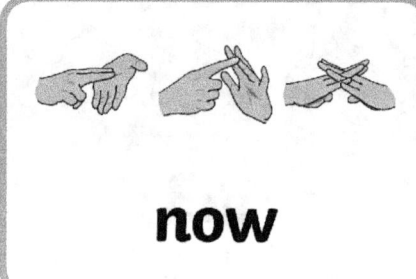
now

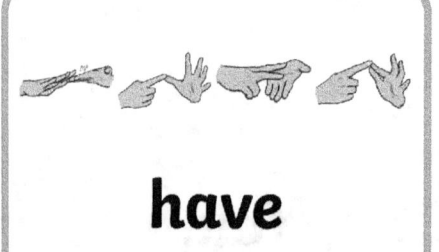
have

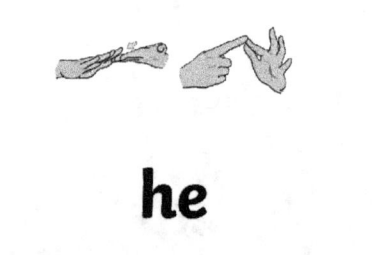
he

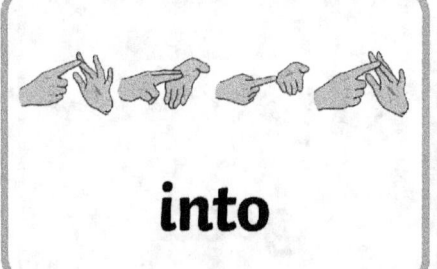
into

like

pretty

ran

ride

saw

on

our

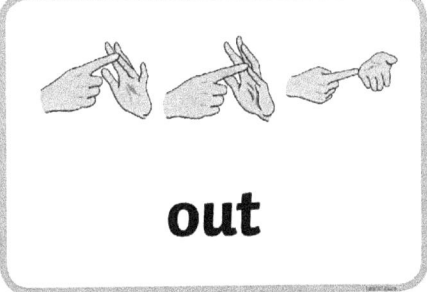
out

please

say

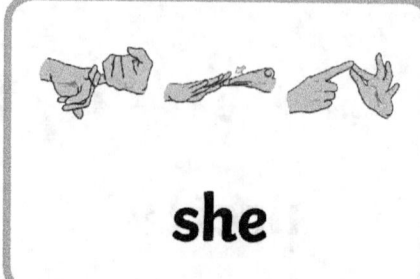
she

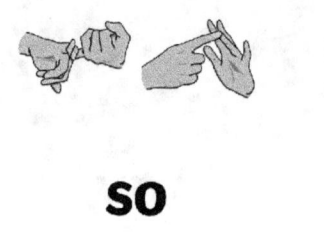
so

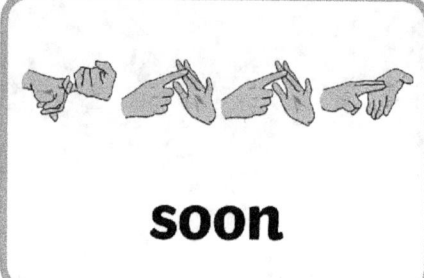
soon

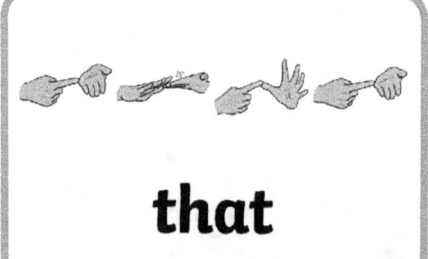
that

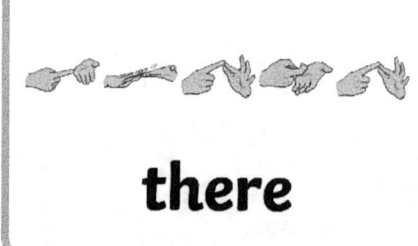
there

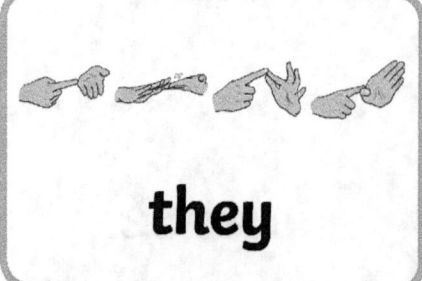
they

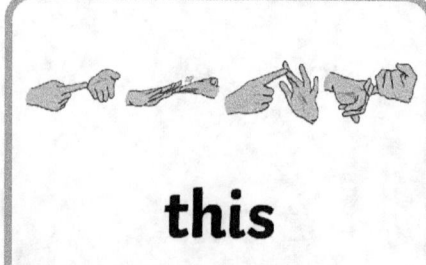
this

**well**

**went**

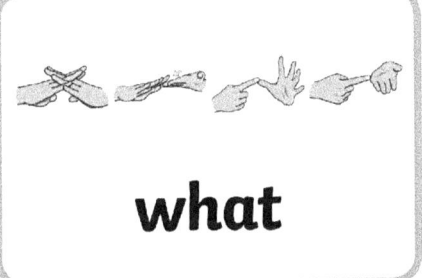

**what**

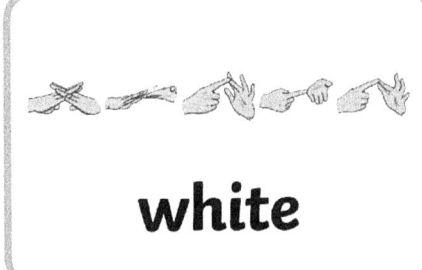

**white**

**too**

**under**

**want**

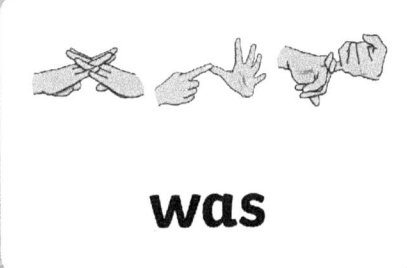

**was**

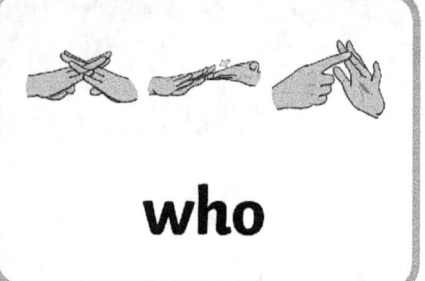

who

will

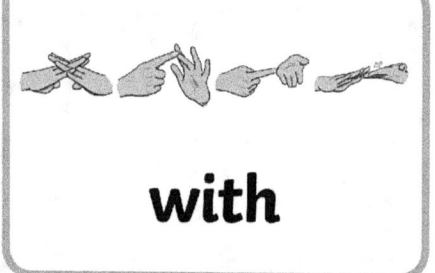

with

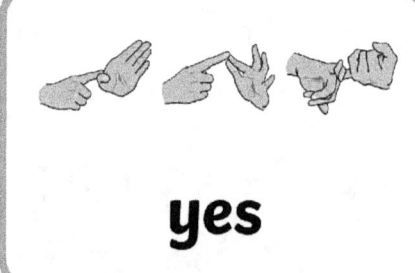

yes

# First Grade Dolch List Sight Words with Fingerspelling

## after

## again

## an

## any

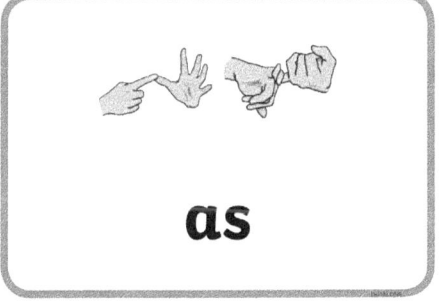

## as

## ask

## by

## could

**every**

**fly**

**from**

**give**

**going**

**had**

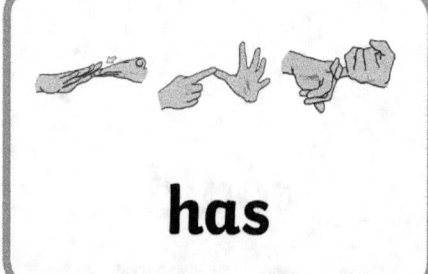
**has**

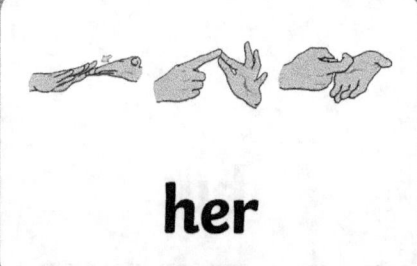
**her**

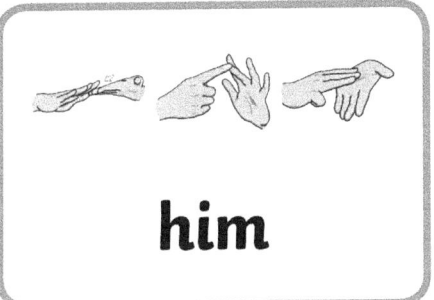
him

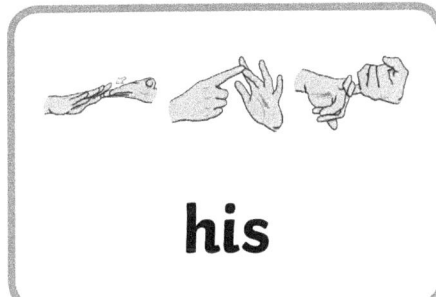
his

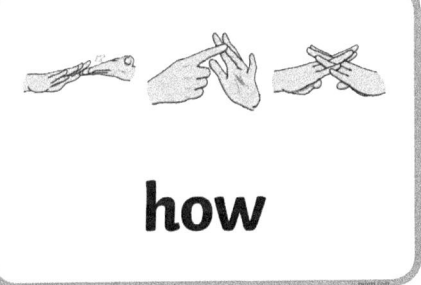
how

just

know

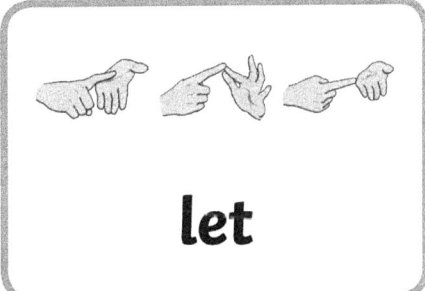
let

live

may

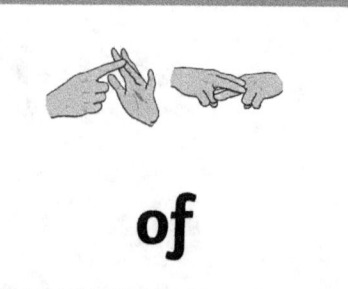
of

old

once

open

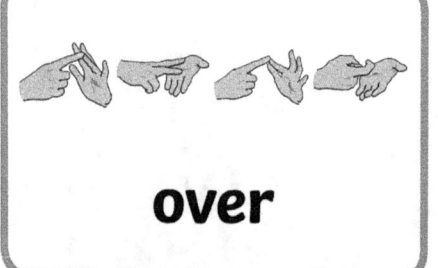
over

put

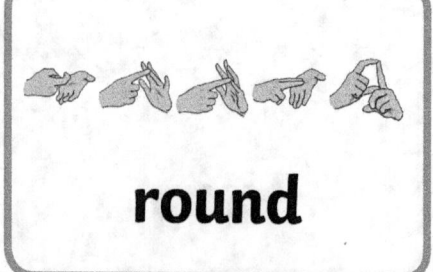
round

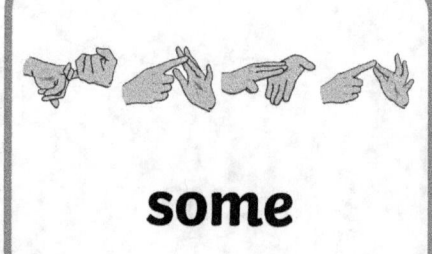
some

 then

 think

 walk

 were

 stop

 take

 thank

 them

# Second Grade Dolch List Sight Words with Fingerspelling

**always**

**around**

**because**

**been**

**before**

**best**

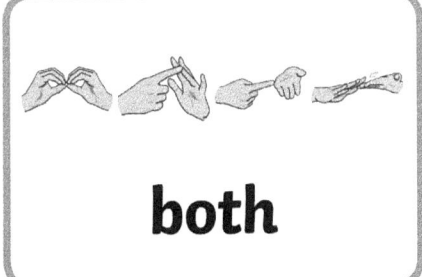

**both**

**buy**

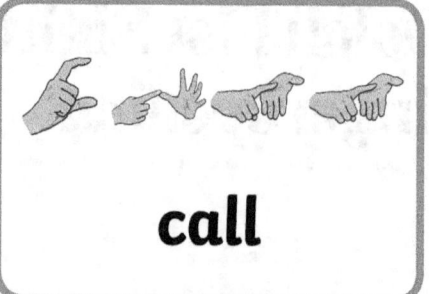
call

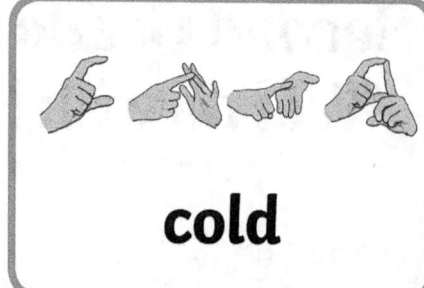
cold

does

don't

fast

first

five

found

gave

goes

green

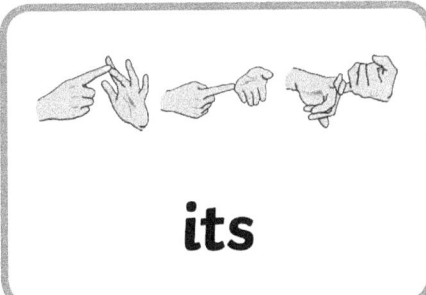

its

made

many

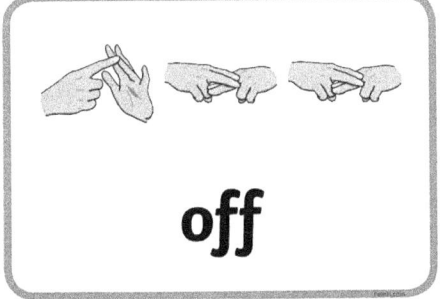

off

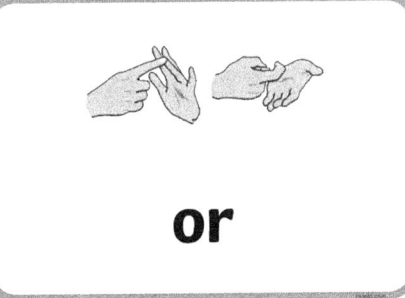

or

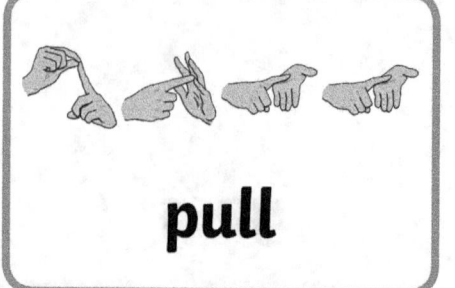
pull

read

right

sing

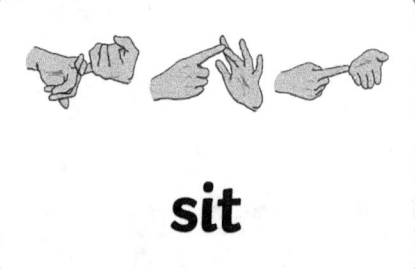
sit

sleep

tell

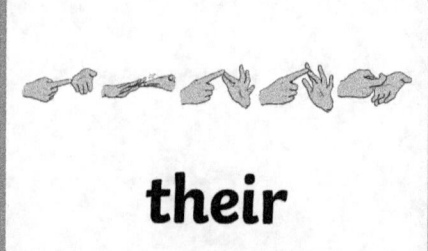
their

these

those

upon

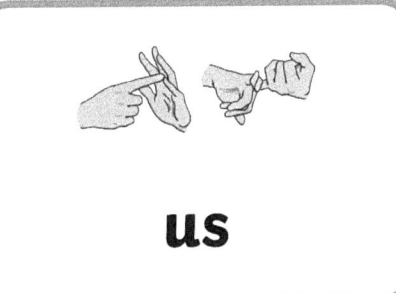
us

use

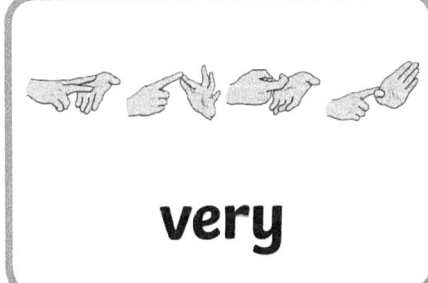
very

wash

which

why

wish

work

would

write

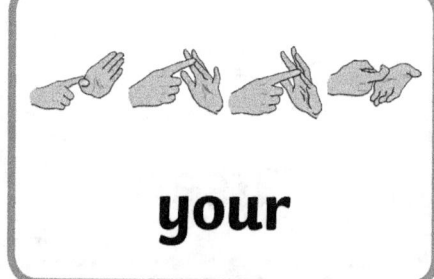
your

# Third Grade Dolch List Sight Words with Fingerspelling

**about**

**better**

**bring**

**carry**

**clean**

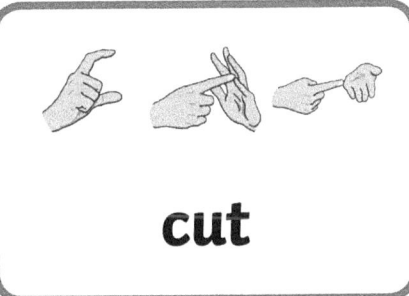
**cut**

**done**

**draw**

drink

eight

fall

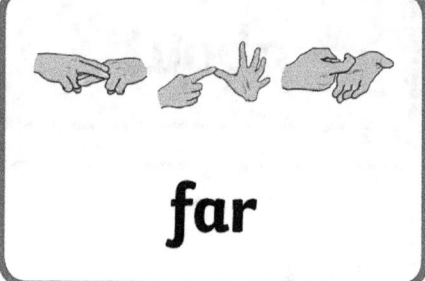
far

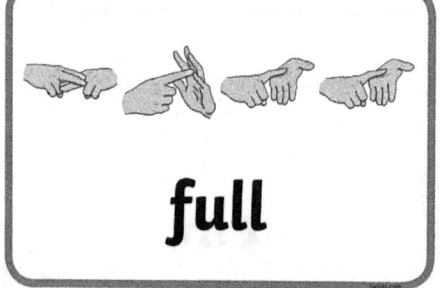
full

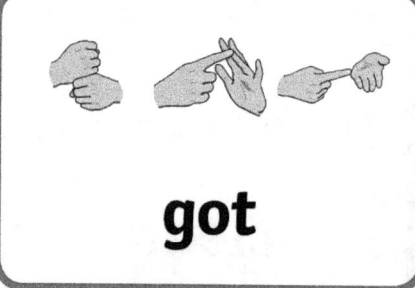
got

grow

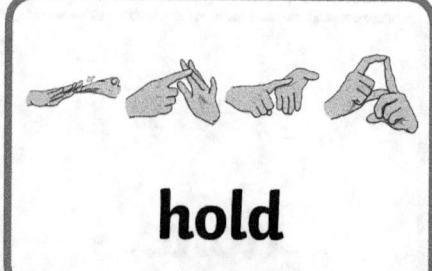
hold

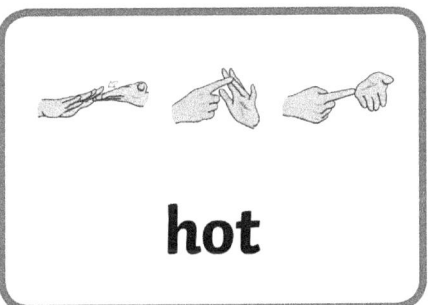

hot

hurt

if

keep

kind

laugh

light

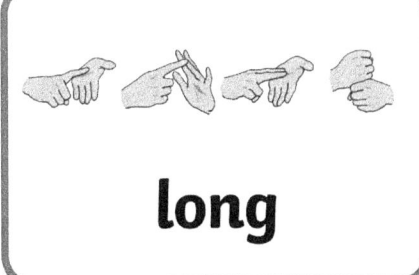

long

**much**

**myself**

**never**

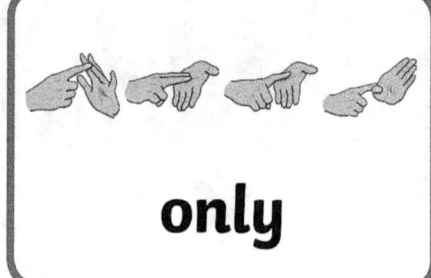

**only**

**own**

**pick**

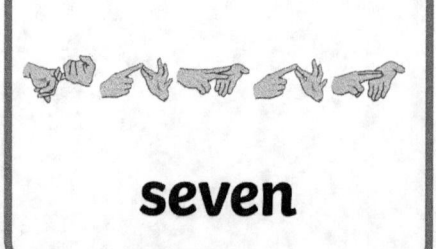

**seven**

**shall**

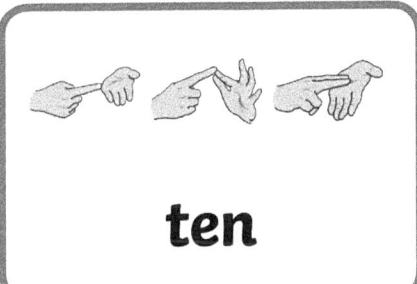
ten

today

together

try

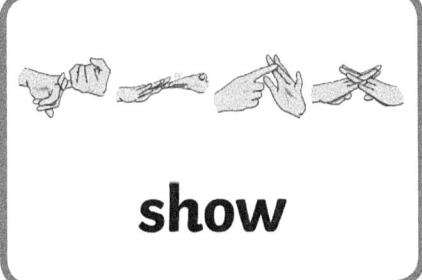
show

six

small

start

# Thank you!
# Please leave a review.

www.ingramcontent.com/pod-product-compliance
Lightning Source LLC
LaVergne TN
LVHW020438080526
838202LV00055B/5254